Ministering to Your Family

A Collection of Sermons

by
Kenneth E. Hagin and Kenneth W. Hagin

Unless otherwise indicated, all Scripture quotations in this volume are from the *King James Version* of the Bible.

Eleventh Printing 2007

ISBN-13: 978-0-89276-407-5
ISBN-10: 0-89276-407-4

In the U.S. write:
Kenneth Hagin Ministries
P.O. Box 50126
Tulsa, OK 74150-0126
1-888-28-FAITH
www.rhema.org

In Canada write:
Kenneth Hagin Ministries
P.O. Box 335, Station D
Etobicoke (Toronto), Ontario
Canada, M9A 4X3
www.rhemacanada.org

Copyright © 1986 RHEMA Bible Church
AKA Kenneth Hagin Ministries, Inc.
All rights reserved.
Printed in USA

The Faith Shield is a trademark of RHEMA Bible Church, AKA Kenneth Hagin Ministries, Inc., registered with the U.S. Patent and Trademark Office and therefore may not be duplicated.

Contents

Chapter 1
On the Matter of a Mate

By Kenneth E. Hagin

In what areas can you exercise faith? What can you believe for?

First, you can believe for everything the Word of God promises you or provides for you. But you can't believe *beyond* the Word. Why not? Because "... *faith cometh by hearing, and hearing by the word of God*" (Rom. 10:17). Faith is based on what God's Word says, and you cannot believe beyond your knowledge of God's Word. If people try to do this, they will get in trouble.

For example, years ago I met a denominational pastor who received the baptism of the Holy Spirit, spoke in tongues, and was kicked out of his denomination.

With no church to pastor, he had gone into business for himself in a large city, and he started attending the largest Full Gospel church in that city. This man was unmarried and was probably between 35 and 40.

He told me that a beautiful woman sang in the church choir, and because "You can have what you say" and "Whatever you desire, just pray and believe you receive," he was going to pray and believe that he was going to get her for a wife.

However, I can't find where the Bible says, "I promise John that he can have Mary for a wife." Mary may not want to be his wife — and John may be just as well off without her anyway!

So I asked the man, "Have you ever talked to this woman? Have you ever had a date with her?"

"No," he replied.

Sitting out there in the congregation while the choir sang on Sunday mornings, this man had seen the woman, was attracted to her, and thought because "You can have what you say," he could just say that they would be married, and it would come to pass.

But under what conditions will it come to pass?

"Well, if I believe it strongly enough," some will argue.

No, faith must be based on God's Word. As we have seen, faith comes by hearing, and hearing by the Word. And the Word of God says, *"Whoso findeth a wife findeth a good thing, and obtaineth favour of the Lord"* (Prov. 18:22).

"Whoso findeth a wife" implies that you have a part to play, all right, but you must be open to the Lord's direction, and you must realize that you cannot go against another person's free will.

The Lord will lead and guide you. You have a right to claim His guidance, because He has promised to guide you. But just to pick somebody out and say, "I'm going to believe God and she's going to be my wife" won't work.

Another's Will Is Involved

The woman you want to marry may not want to be your wife. That would work the other way around for women: The man you want to marry may not want to be your husband.

Friends, you're not going to be able to override another person's will in the matter, so you may as well settle that once and for all.

God Himself does not exercise authority over human spirits. If He did, He'd make everybody in the world get saved today, and then we could enter into the Millennium.

We only have authority over evil spirits; *not* over human spirits. God has granted mankind free will to choose for themselves.

In the first meeting I held after leaving my last pastorate, an unmarried woman in her thirties asked me, "Brother Hagin, do I have the right to believe for a husband?"

"I believe you do," I replied, "because the Bible says, *'Whoso findeth a WIFE findeth a good thing, and obtaineth favour of the Lord'* — and it would be a poor rule that wouldn't work both ways."

Will faith work here?

I told the young woman, "You can't just pick out somebody and say, 'That one's mine.' But you can ask God to lead you. You can claim a mate by faith and let God work out the details because you believe Him."

Standing in Faith

For many months, it didn't look like things were going to work for this young woman: No young man came into her life. Every time I saw her, I encouraged her to stand in faith. She would say, "I'm standing in faith. It's going to work. I know it is!" She had certain ideals in mind. She said, "I'm not a minister myself, but I have been in the work of the Lord for many years, and I want to marry a minister."

In the process of time, I saw her, and she had married a fine man — a minister. Her faith had worked.

I also remember two beautiful young women who attended a revival meeting I once conducted in Oklahoma.

They had just graduated from high school with the highest grades in their class. Both were saved and baptized in the Holy Spirit in my meeting. Some months later, when I returned to that church for another meeting, the Lord led me to minister a word of wisdom to one of the girls.

Afterwards, the pastor said, "Brother Hagin, I'm so glad you did that. You didn't know this, I'm sure, but that young woman is engaged to be married, and we're concerned about it. The young man has attended church here, but I'll just be honest with you — I'm sure he pretended he got saved so he could marry her."

Something Better

I hadn't known these details the night the Lord had me minister to the young woman. She was sitting on the front row that night. I asked the congregation to sing, because I didn't want everyone to hear what I told her. I said to her, "The Lord told me to tell you this: 'I've got something better for you. Don't marry right now. I've got something better for you.' "

Two years later I was out in California in a campmeeting when a fine-looking young couple came up to me. The woman said, "Brother Hagin, do you remember me?"

"No," I said, "but your face looks familiar."

She told me her name, but I still couldn't remember who she was.

"Well," she said, "you'll remember this: You called me up while the congregation was singing and you told me the Lord said not to marry then because He had something better for me."

"Oh," I said. "I remember that."

"Well," she said happily, "here he is!"

Then she told me she and her husband were in Bible college preparing for the ministry. "Oh, I'm so glad the Lord arrested me and ministered to me," she said. "I would have made a fatal mistake. We're so happy. And we're working for God."

God did have something better for her. God can lead and guide us. We need to be open to the leading of God.

You see, *we can believe God and exercise faith for anything that is promised in the Bible.* But we must base our faith upon what God's Word says. If we get into areas beyond the Word, we will get into gray areas — into dark areas. As long as we're in the Word, we're in the light. Then we're on safe ground — sure ground.

Some may say, "I don't know just what direction to take in life, so what shall I believe for?"

Well, trust God for guidance, because He has promised to guide you. Claim His guidance by faith. Say, "The Lord is guiding me. He is leading me. I may not see it this moment. I may not even know what to do at the moment. But He is my Guide, and I am trusting Him."

"For as many as are led by the Spirit of God, they are the sons of God" (Rom. 8:14). God will guide you. But remember that He leads you just one step at a time.

Chapter 2
Ministering in Our Own World

By Kenneth Hagin Jr.

And he said unto them, Go ye into all the world, and preach the gospel to every creature.

— Mark 16:15

Then saith he unto his disciples, The harvest truly is plenteous, but the labourers are few.

— Matthew 9:37

But ye shall receive power, after that the Holy Ghost is come upon you: and ye shall be witnesses unto me both in Jerusalem, and in all Judaea, and in Samaria, and unto the uttermost part of the earth.

— Acts 1:8

The word "world" can mean many different things. We can say "world" and mean the entire planet that we live on. Or "world" may mean the environment we live in — our community, our home.

Now, it's not difficult to get most Christians excited about traveling somewhere else to minister, but don't talk to them about ministering at home!

However, if you're ever going to be used by God to minister in the uttermost parts of the earth, you'd better be able to minister at home first. God can't and won't use you if you can't minister at home.

In Acts 1:8, Jesus told His disciples to minister in Judaea. That was the state in which they lived. Notice the statement Jesus made next. He said they were to minister in Samaria. That's the place they hated most. As you study Jewish history, you will learn that the Jews utterly hated the Samaritans. They called them dogs.

Notice that Jesus said *first* of all, start ministering at home — in your own state. *Then* go to the place you hate the most. *Then* go to the uttermost parts of the earth.

Isn't it strange how we always want to turn the Bible around? We want to go to the uttermost parts of the earth *first*. The *last* place we want to minister is at home. But I'll tell you one thing: Your testimony is not much good if it isn't accepted by your own hometown people!

Yes, we need to minister to the world, but what world do we need to minister to? Let's minister first in *our own world*, our home.

Christian homes are being attacked today by the devil as never before. He's tearing Christian homes apart. We need to begin to minister to our own world, to our own household.

Do you know how to minister to your own household without a lot of fanfare? It's simply by having daily devotions in your home and by living a consistent Christian life.

Don't throw a fit one day and let your children get away with the same things the next. Don't preach one thing and act like something else at home. Don't talk to your family about living for God and then all of a sudden get angry and slam your fist through the wall. (I know that happens in some people's homes!)

Yes, you can ask God to forgive you, and He will forgive you. But you've made a damaging impression on your child, and you also need to talk with your child and apologize for your behavior.

The Charismatic Home

In our charismatic world, the father of the family is out taking care of his business, and the mother is busy going to all those prayer meetings, trying to win the rest of the world to the Lord. The children are being neglected. They're insecure. That isn't right, and I can prove it by the Word of God.

Some women will argue, "Yes, but Pastor Hagin, God called me to minister. And as soon as I get my husband off to work and my children off to school, I've got to go out and minister."

But what happens when your husband comes home and the house looks like a pigpen because it hasn't been cleaned? The bed hasn't been made in three days, because you haven't had time; you've been out preaching. I can prove by the Word of God that the highest calling you have is to take care of the house and take care of those children God gave you. Your first ministry is to them.

After you minister in your household, *then* you can go out, if you have time left over, and do something for God.

On the other hand, men, don't leave the house at 6 a.m. and get home at 11 p.m. and expect your wife and family to treat you very well, because you're neglecting *your* duties.

I'm not a women's libber, and I'm not on the other side of the fence into the extreme submission teaching. I'm not for all this liberty on the one hand, or all this extreme submission on the other hand. You will find from the Word of God that God designed the home with man and woman standing side by side and ministering together.

When I marry a couple, I always tell them that woman was not taken out of man's feet to be trampled on by him. She was not taken out of his head to be dominated by him. She was taken out of his rib, next to his heart, to stand beside him so they could enjoy love, unity, and harmony together. When you understand that, you have understood the correct Biblical viewpoint of marriage.

True Biblical Submission

One day at Rhema, a young woman came up to me and said, "I don't feel like I ought to be in school. My husband said I had to come, so I submitted to him and came. But I've got a 2 year old and a 3 year old at home. I have to go home after school and try to study and try to take care of everything else. I just don't think I ought to be here, but I'm supposed to submit to my husband. He is the head of the house."

That's a lot of nonsense. Submission is right and true when it's Biblical, but not when it's like that.

The teaching of extreme submission is part of what's tearing up homes and churches today.

Men do have spiritual authority in the home — but it's not just by yelling, "Bless God, you're going to do it because *I* said do it!" You big bullies! You can make anybody do anything you want them to — your wife, your children, and others — but one of these days that son of yours is going to grow up. He's going to stand about as tall as you are, look you in the eye, and say, "You aren't making me do anything anymore!"

Learn how to put your home together properly. Parents, don't talk about all the church people in front of your children. As far as my children know, all the preachers and church members our family knows are the greatest people in the world. We never discuss ministry-related problems in front of our children.

I'm appalled at people who try to minister to somebody else when their own home is in turmoil. The Apostle Paul said that if you can't manage your own home, you don't have any right ministering (1 Tim. 3:4,5). I'm not talking about ministering solely from the platform; I'm talking about ministering in the local body too.

When you minister effectively at home, and get everything there in the right order, then you can begin to go out and minister to the world.

Ministry in the Local Church

The second "world" where you need to minister is your local church or fellowship; the local body where you attend. And if you don't attend a local church or fellowship regularly, you're not living in line with the Word of God. The Bible says, *"Not forsaking the assembling of ourselves together, as the manner of some is; but exhorting one another: and so much the more, as ye see the day approaching"* (Heb. 10:25).

You won't get involved just staying home watching services on television. You'll sit there in your easy chair and doze off, not hearing half of what's going on.

You should be involved with a local church where the Full Gospel is taught and preached. You should be involved by attending, by giving tithes and offerings, and by working at whatever needs to be done.

A pastor can't do it all. He needs some help in

ministering salvation and healing for physical needs as well
as for the brokenhearted, the bruised, the oppressed, and
the lonely who are sitting there in that congregation.

We need to be sensitive enough to the Spirit of God
to sense the hurts and the needs of the person sitting next
to us in church, and to minister to him or her. We need
to realize that we're living in a world that's hurting. That
world needs to be ministered to!

But to minister, we need to get back to the basics —
back to commitment and rededication to God. Matthew
6:33 says, *"But seek ye first the kingdom of God, and his
righteousness; and all these things shall be added unto
you."*

There are too many people seeking the "things" — the
airplanes, the cars, the houses, and all that. I believe we
can have "things," because God's Word says we can, but
we shouldn't seek them. We should seek the kingdom of
God!

When we get interested in getting people saved and
healed, the "things" will be added — the things we want,
need, and desire. Our problem is that we're seeking the
things instead of the kingdom.

I don't know how many services I've been to where
they preached prosperity and faith, but no altar call was
given. There wasn't one person prayed for, for healing. If
there was any praying at all, it was, "God bless me and
my finances." That's part of it, but that's not the bottom
line.

*The bottom line is getting people SAVED from SIN
and getting them on the road to heaven.* All our other
blessings are luxuries!

Thank God for the baptism in the Holy Spirit. Thank

God for healing. Thank God for meeting all our needs. But did you know that none of these blessings are necessary for our getting into the kingdom of God? The only thing that's necessary is being born again by the blood of the Lord Jesus Christ. That's a *necessity*. Everything else we get from God is a *luxury*.

One day as I was praying, the Lord said to me, "Why do you think I taught people how to use their faith to get things they want?"

"I don't know."

"Because," He said, "people want things for themselves, and that is the best way to teach them how to use their faith. They know how to believe God to get what they need. *Now I want them to take that same faith and begin to believe souls into the kingdom.*"

Have you ever been to one of our large crusades? Have you ever noticed that, whether we preach a salvation message or not, we always give an altar call, and there are always many people who come forward for salvation? Do you know why? Because Brother Hagin takes the same faith that he uses to believe for the finances of the meeting and believes for the salvation of people. That's the bottom line — salvation.

People are hurting! Let's get back to the basics. Let's get back to dedicating ourselves to what God actually called us to do in the first place: Be witnesses of Jesus Christ!

Chapter 3
The Role of the Christian Father

By Kenneth Hagin Jr.

When you study the Word of God, you will find that God has much to say about the care of the family.

Personally, I believe that the Bible teaches that we are to take care of our families *first* — before all of our other obligations. For example, in First Timothy 5:8 we read, *"But if any provide not for his own, and specially for those of his own house, he hath denied the faith, and is worse than an infidel."*

But caring for a family involves more than just providing food, shelter, and clothing. It also involves giving love, discipline, and time to family members. Remember, your children don't learn just from your words; they also learn from your actions and attitudes. And they can't pick up their parents' actions or attitudes if their parents are absent from the home!

How To Lose Your Family

My dad, Kenneth E. Hagin, believes that unless it is a life-or-death situation, as it was with him, you should not leave your family behind to go into the full-time traveling ministry. The quickest way to lose your family is to go on the road and stay on the road!

Yes, it is commendable to throw yourself into your ministry, but I have seen ministers do this and lose those who were precious and dear to them. These ministers never learned how to set priorities in their lives.

I believe that the minister's personal relationship with

God, his spouse, their *children*, and the *call* of God on the minister's life are to be ranked *in that order.*

Ministers *must* work out a schedule by which all of these responsibilities can be met. It will take work, diplomacy, and supernatural wisdom to meet all these responsibilities successfully.

If your family suffers because of your call, or if your call suffers because of your family, you've got a problem. There will be times when you may have to be gone from home — I grant you that — but there will be other times when your family must come first.

Children need to grow up in a stable atmosphere where they can have friends and be involved in normal social activities. Their social life should not suffer because of your call to the ministry!

When our son, Craig, started school, our daughter, Denise, was only 2, but she cried to go to school like "Bubbie." A church near our home had a "Mother's Day Out" program, so Lynette enrolled Denise in it, and she loved it. However, Denise found out that one of her little friends there was enrolled in an afternoon class so, of course, Denise wanted to go with her friend. We allowed her to do so.

Each May, Denise's class gave a recital. One year I had already set up my summer speaking schedule when I learned that Denise's recital would occur the day before I was to speak in a certain large city. I called my crusade director and instructed him either to change the meeting date, or, if that was impossible, to cancel it entirely.

Some people may say, "Somebody could go to hell because you didn't hold that service!"

But did you ever stop to think that if you win the whole

world and lose your family, you haven't really accomplished anything?

My first responsibility is to my family. It was very important to that little girl that her daddy be at her recital each year — so I was.

Nobody Cared About Curtis

It isn't only preachers who get so involved in their work that their children suffer. I've seen people in other lines of work who just don't care about what is important to their children.

Before our children were in grade school, I coached track. Some of the parents never came to any event. Their children would work so hard, running track every afternoon to prepare for the meets, but the parents never bothered to attend.

One little red-headed boy by the name of Curtis trained especially hard. He couldn't run fast, but he was good at running long distance, and he ran every day.

I once said to him, "Curtis, you don't have a chance in anything except the long-distance run. But you can win the city championship in the mile run if you'll practice. While I'm working with the rest of the guys in the broad jump, the high jump, and the hurdles, you run laps."

Curtis won the preliminary mile run hands down, but his dad and mother were not there. The city meet was scheduled around Eastertime. Curtis' parents called me and said, "Curtis won't be at the meet. We're going to his grandma's." I said, "Well, let him stay with me (he was crying and he wanted to stay home and compete). He's a good runner. He can win city." They refused. Later they decided not to go out of town after all, but even then they didn't come to see their son run.

Curtis won the city meet easily. And the only adults who praised him were the school principal and I.

I watched Curtis through the years. By the time he had entered junior high school, he wasn't involved in anything anymore. Do you know why? *Because nobody cared!*

Yet Curtis was a boy who had ability. He wasn't fast, but he could set a pace all day long and never give up. He could outrun the competition. But he received no love at home. His parents wouldn't make any effort to get up early on a Saturday morning to encourage him in this sport.

Work at Your Relationships

It's not easy holding a three-day meeting, rushing to the plane still in your dress clothes, flying all night with little rest on "the red-eye special," and then changing into jeans as soon as you get home in order to spend the day with your family. After all that, you would prefer to head for your favorite chair, turn on "Wide World of Sports," and doze and relax. But to win your children, you must put forth the effort necessary to build a close relationship with them. It takes *time* to build relationships. It takes *effort* to get involved with your children's activities after spending a long day at work. It takes *sacrifices* on the parents' part to put the children's interests first.

In a typical working day, I will teach, run the ministry, pastor Rhema Bible Church, deal with people's problems, and answer hundreds of pieces of mail and memos. Usually I stay at the office until about 5 p.m. When I get home, my mind is tired. I don't want any noise or activity. All

I want to do is to eat, change into jogging pants and a T-shirt, and do absolutely nothing!

But I've got a son, a daughter, and a wife. I make it a point to sit down and listen to my children — to get involved. Some people sit down with their children, but they never get involved with them. When a child has a problem, to that child it is as big as a mountain. If I shut my children out of my world, I'm giving the devil an opportunity to get in.

One Saturday afternoon several years ago, my son got an old kite out of the closet and was trying to get it to fly. He came in the house and asked me for help. I could have said, "Well, Craig, Dad is going to have a hard week next week. I've only got two days in the office, and then I've got to go out of town to preach. I need to relax right now." But that wouldn't have sufficed. So I got up from watching television and we went to the store and bought a new kite. And then we went down to the school yard and flew the kite.

My wife has made similar sacrifices. Once Lynette was scheduled to accompany me to a meeting in Houston. One of the children said, "Mommy, please don't go this time." Lynette didn't go. She shed a few tears over it, because we hadn't been together by ourselves for a long time. Staying home that time was a real sacrifice on her part, but her dedication to those children has paid off in the long run.

Sometimes you must put your children's activities first. You may have to give up something you want to do so that they can participate in a program at church, for example. It is important for children to be active in a spiritual atmosphere. Children need that identification with a local church.

Charismatics' Children

Many charismatics have insecure children. This is simply because they are putting everything else ahead of their children. You may win five hundred million people to God, but it will count exactly zero if you lose the three or four souls in your own home. According to the Word of God, your first responsibility is to your children.

The Bible says, *"Train up a child in the way he should go: and when he is old, he will not depart from it"* (Prov. 22:6). Think about the definition of the word "train." How much training can take place if you are not home?

Some years ago, I took two overseas missionary trips without my family. In discussing going a third time, I said, "Unless my family can go with me, I'm not going."

My little girl had cried herself to sleep the last time I was gone. She was all right for the first few days, but after that, she began to miss her daddy, because I tuck her into bed every night. Children can understand your being gone somewhat — but you've got to realize that they're still children. You don't know exactly how those little minds think. Denise started saying, "I understand that people need to be preached to, and they need to be healed — but I need my daddy too." When you hear things like that, you'd better stop and think! You're on the verge of losing someone in your own household!

Picking Up the Signals

Now, sometimes your wife may say, "You've been gone a lot lately, and we haven't had much time together." You had better begin to pick up on statements like that. It may be time for you to take a trip together for a few days. Your wife is trying to tell you, "I need you." You'd better learn to look at her and know when she needs you. Pick up on the little things. At different times, each of the marriage partners needs special love and support from the other one. Learn to give the support that is needed.

If the husband is out traveling a lot, the wife had better realize his needs and meet them at home. The devil has a lot of traps set for him out there, and it is easier for him to fall into them when he hasn't been taken care of at home. I'm just dealing with some down-to-earth facts here. God ordained the union of the man and the woman. Let's learn how to live according to His plan.

Yes, you have a ministry and you have to reach the world, but you have to think of your wife and children first.

'Little Pitchers'

Here's another important point to remember: Don't talk negatively in front of your children about the churches you've visited, the meetings you've held, or other preachers' problems. People who do, give children the wrong idea. Words said in the home can come back to haunt you! Children will reflect your thinking. They will say what you say.

Therefore, it is important for the children's sake that you always keep before them the thought that ministers are excellent people. If you train children properly, they will be able to handle truths later on when they have to face them.

My wife and I talk about any problems in the ministry

just between ourselves. As far as the children are concerned, every Rhema student is perfect; every church member is perfect; and every preacher we know is perfect. We never discuss our office business in front of them, either. The only thing we talk about is, "Let's get together and believe God for Rhema's finances; for buildings, and so forth." *Don't burden your children's little ears and minds with adult problems!*

Why Preachers' Kids Fall Away

I have known many preachers' children who are not Christians today. They don't even go to church. Why? Because their daddy was always too busy with Johnny Brown and Katie Jones and Charlie Smith at the church to give his own children the time of day. So his children became bitter and resentful, and they turned their backs on the things of God.

Some of these preachers have talked to my dad and said, "We thought God *required* this of us. We thought we were *supposed* to give up our own family, and let them get by the best way they could. We gave ourselves entirely to the church, and now we've lost our own family!"

That's an indictment, and it hurts. I've seen men weep as they told Dad this. But they didn't have to neglect their family and ultimately lose them — it wasn't necessary. They needed to spend time with their wife and children.

Many ministers have lost their wives because of the demands of the ministry. They may not be legally divorced — they may share the same house — but they don't have a marriage. Their marriage is just two people living under the same roof. I know pastors who have slept in separate bedrooms from their wives for years. They don't argue or fuss. They came to an understanding a long time ago. They don't want to ruin the ministry, so they continue to stay married.

That kind of life is not necessary if you work at your marriage. God does not require so much of you that He asks you to destroy your marriage relationship — not when it was God who established the marriage relationship in the first place! Neither does God require you to raise insecure children who get mad at God because they think He took their daddy or mother away from them all the time!

Fathers, if you're out on the road preaching during the summer, take your son with you. Go to the meetings together. Yes, it will be difficult. You may not have as much time to study — but taking him along is important. You're building a relationship.

Unless you develop the proper relationship when your children are younger, you're not going to develop it when they get older.

It's Your Responsibility

I believe that the Word of God teaches that your wife and children are your primary responsibility, even over and above your ministry. Those children did not ask to be brought into this world. You and your partner brought them into this world, and God tells you it is your responsibility to raise them in the paths of righteousness and godliness.

It's not the responsibility of a baby-sitter, or a grandmother, or Aunt Susie. I don't care how much others may love your children — they cannot give them what you can give them.

It's time to realize that God does not expect us to shirk our responsibilities in one area and to pick up another responsibility somewhere else. Sometimes the call must come first and the family second — but not all the time. Let that circle rotate, and bring the family up on top the next time. Learn how to let it be a natural rotation: call, wife, children — all centered around God.

Then you will find that you are living a happy, well-balanced family life. Your call will balance itself out. This won't happen, however, without work, tears, and dedication on your part.

I've shed a few tears over having to leave my family and go preach. I'm dedicated to the call — but I'm just as dedicated to them. There are times I must preach, but there are other times when I let invitations to preach slide by so that I can be with my family. In other words, I don't preach every time I get an invitation.

Seeing a Sermon

My son and daughter need to see me choosing priorities and living life to its fullest. I can talk about it until I'm blue in the face, but my children need to *see* — not just *hear about* — me doing it. (They also will see God's love at the heart of my decisions.) Then I will never have to worry about them turning away from God when they get older.

By learning to mesh your call and your family life, you will find that your life becomes well rounded. Your call, wife, and children will rotate naturally, all centered around God.

Your children will see you living the Christian life — not saying one thing and doing another. And although this kind of lifestyle takes dedication to achieve, you will find that life will become beautiful as you learn to keep the proper balance between your family life and your call of God to minister.

Chapter 4
Surrounding a Teenager
With Faith and Love

By Kenneth E. Hagin

. . . he shall have whatsoever he saith.

— Mark 11:23

What are you going to have in life?

What you say.

Who said that?

Jesus said it.

Is it true? Do you suppose Jesus really knew what He was talking about? I believe He told the truth, don't you?

Well, if Jesus told the truth, I'd better check up on what I'm saying; especially if I'm not satisfied with what I have. And I'm not just talking about being healed.

At a Full Gospel Business Men's Convention in a certain large city, a woman came up to me after one of the afternoon teaching sessions. She said, "Brother Hagin, I want you to promise me something."

I replied, "Well, I want to find out what it is first."

A Mother's Request

She said, "I want you to promise me that you'll pray every day for my son. He's 15 years old. I'm a widow, and I can't do a thing in the world with him. I can't get him to go to church. He's in with a gang, and I'm afraid they're on drugs. He's out until 3 and 4 o'clock in the morning. I lie awake nights waiting for the phone to ring telling me they've got him down at the jail."

I interrupted her before she could tell any more about how bad her son was. I said to her, "I'm not going to do it."

That shocked her.

"You're not?"

"No, ma'am. I'm not. I won't promise you I'll pray for him at all."

"Well!" she said.

"You see," I continued, "in the first place, it wouldn't do any good, because you'd nullify the effects of my prayers by your wrong believing and your wrong talking. No matter how many people pray, as long as you keep telling your son that he'll never amount to anything and he'll wind up in reform school and the penitentiary — he'll never make it."

Her eyes got big. "How did you know I was talking that way to him?"

Products of Words

I said, "To be in the mess he's in, you had to talk him into it. We're products of words. Children are products of words. Words will make a boy love an education. Words will make a boy want to go to church, or they'll keep him out of church."

"What should I do?" the woman asked.

"In the first place, since you've done this so long, and because he's as old as he is, just leave him alone. He resents your talking to him and trying to tell him anything. Just leave him alone. Don't tell him anything. Don't preach at him. Don't nag him.

"Now for the second thing," I went on, "change your thinking and change your talking. At home, even when you don't know where your son is, say, 'I surround my son with faith.' You have been surrounding him with doubt. Now surround him with faith. And say, even if your heart doesn't believe it to begin with — say it out of your mouth, and once it registers on your heart you will start believing — 'I do not believe he's going to the reform school. I do not believe he's going to the penitentiary. I believe he's coming to God. I believe _____' and state what you believe."

"Well," she said, "I'll try it."

"It won't work. It won't work if you *try* it. But it will work if you'll *do* it. Jesus didn't say we would have whatever we *tried;* He said we'd have whatever we *said.*"

That convention was in August. The Full Gospel Business Men had another convention in that city the next year in October, fourteen months later, and I returned to speak again.

After the afternoon service, a woman came up to me and said, "Brother Hagin, do you remember me?"

"No, I meet so many people I don't really remember you."

"Oh," she said, "remember when you were here August a year ago and I asked you to pray for my boy, and you shocked me by saying you wouldn't?"

A Good Report

The woman continued, "I want to tell you one thing: What you told me works! Now, it didn't look like it was going to work. My son got worse. And keeping my mouth shut was the hardest thing I ever did. But I kept saying — every day I said it, every night I said it — 'I surround him with faith and love. I believe he's coming to God. I believe things are going to work out right in his life. I believe he's not going to reform school.'

"My head said that was where he was going because of the bunch he was running around with, but I said from my heart, 'He's not going to the reform school. I do not believe he'll wind up in the penitentiary.' "

She continued, "We went along that way for nearly a year. Then one Sunday morning, after he'd been out nearly all night, he got up. Ordinarily, he would have slept in, but he got up and came to the breakfast table. And while we were eating, he said, 'Momma, I believe I'll go to Sunday School with you this morning.' "

She said, "I just acted nonchalantly and said, 'Now, son, you were up awfully late; you probably need the rest.' " (Before, she had been nagging him to go.)

"No," he said, "I want to go."

"Well," she said. "It's up to you, but you only got a few hours sleep."

"I want to go," he said. And he went to Sunday School and stayed for church.

"The very next Sunday morning," the mother told me, "he was out till 4 o'clock in the morning, but again he was up for breakfast."

"Momma," he said to her, "I believe I'll go to Sunday School with you this morning."

She said, "Son, you were out late last night. You need the rest, you know."

"Well, yes," he said, "but I can go. I'm going."

Her son went to Sunday School, stayed for church, and that evening he said to her, "I believe I'll go back with you tonight." When the invitation was given at the end of that service, the young man went to the altar and was saved.

A Brand-New Son

"Since then," she told me, "he's been filled with the Spirit. Just like he was all out for the devil before, now he's all out for God! He's on fire for God! I believe he's going to turn into a preacher! I'll tell you, he's just a brand-new boy. I've got a brand-new boy!

"Thank you," she said. "At first I almost got my feelings hurt; you were so blunt with me. But I saw it. I corrected myself, and, thank God, I've got a brand-new son.

"You know," she added, "I'll tell you something else. He's got a brand-new Momma."

This woman was saved and filled with the Holy Spirit and had been attending a Full Gospel church for years, but she told me that day, "I don't think anymore like I used to think. I almost pinch myself sometimes and say, 'Is this really me?' I used to worry, worry, worry, worry. Now I don't worry anymore.

"Not only that," she continued, "but I feel so good physically. I feel like a young girl. I've got vim, vigor, and vitality."

When this woman began to say the right thing, it worked for her. Jesus said, ". . . *he shall have whatsoever he SAITH.*"

Chapter 5
How To Win Your
Unsaved Loved Ones

By Kenneth E. Hagin

One of the questions most frequently asked of me is how to get unsaved loved ones saved. This is my advice to you.

First, realize that the Father draws people through the Holy Spirit. When the Word of God is preached, the Holy Spirit brings conviction upon people through the Word.

Jesus said, *"No man can come to me, except the Father which hath sent me draw him: and I will raise him up at the last day"* (John 6:44).

Second, pray that God will send someone across your unsaved loved one's path. Jesus said in Matthew 9, *"Pray ye therefore the Lord of the harvest, that he will send forth labourers into his harvest"* (v. 38). We will study more about this later.

I don't believe, however, that there are any rules you can establish in soul-winning that will work for everyone. God might lead one person one way and another person another way. We must always bear in mind the vital work of the Holy Spirit in drawing people to Christ.

Sometimes the members of your family are the most difficult people to deal with. They won't listen to you. Generally speaking, it is better for you *not* to try to deal with them. Now don't misunderstand me — sometimes the Spirit of God may lead you differently. I'm just laying down some general principles here.

How My Family Was Won

I was a teenager when I became born again. Some of my family members were what we call nominal Christians. They knew Jesus was their Savior, but they didn't know much beyond that. I was led by the Spirit of God never to mention anything to them about salvation — and that leading extended to other relatives, like aunts, uncles, and cousins.

One way the Holy Spirit leads us is by an inward witness or inward conviction. I just had the conviction in my spirit that if my relatives saw reality in my life, they would all want it. (That's true in the natural realm too. If you know somebody has a good recipe, for example, you want it.)

According to the Word of God, "...*bodily exercise profiteth little: but GODLINESS IS PROFITABLE unto all things...*" (1 Tim. 4:8). "Profitable" means that it pays off. Paul continued in verse fifteen, *"Meditate upon these things...that thy PROFITING may appear to all."*

So I never said one word about the Lord to any of my close relatives, and I never asked any of them to be saved. I started preaching as a 17-year-old boy, but I never asked my relatives to come hear me preach. They came, but I never asked them. I never said one word to any of them about salvation. Why? I was led not to. I knew in my spirit that I shouldn't.

Don't Nag

Too often people nag their unsaved relatives until they don't even like you to be around them. Through the years when we went to family Thanksgiving or Christmas get-togethers, I tried to enter into their normal activities and games.

Before I was converted and began to preach, my family never prayed at the table, but afterwards, they always asked me to say grace. I never said anything else to them.

But one thing about it: *Through the years, every one of them got born again!*

I have noticed that the two most common mistakes people make in dealing with their families are these: (1) They try to be super-spiritual, and (2) They overdo witnessing.

Yes, the Bible teaches witnessing, but you have to realize that there's an old proverb that says, "What you *are* speaks so loud I can't hear what you say." People who do a lot of talking may not have enough life to back up their witness.

The Greatest Witness

I just let my life witness — and my relatives eventually all wanted the Lord. They saw something in my life that they wanted. I think that's the greatest witness, actually. If you live the Christian life in front of people, it will influence your spouse, your children, and your other relatives.

Even though I did not *witness* to my relatives, I did *pray* for them through the years. I prayed for one man in particular who was going through some severe tests in his family.

One day I was in my hometown on some business, and I happened to see a familiar figure walking down the street.

This person's walk reminded me of that relative. As I pulled alongside the man, however, I decided he was the wrong person, so I drove on by.

After I had gone several blocks, it suddenly hit me: Momma had said this relative had lost about 50 pounds and I wouldn't even recognize him anymore. I hadn't; he looked so haggard.

I quickly said out loud, "Dear God, save So-and-so."

A voice in the back seat of my car said, "Well, that's what I'm *trying* to do!" The voice was so clear, I looked around to see if somebody had hid back there! Then I knew something instantly: I was wasting my time praying such a prayer for that person's salvation, because God had been trying to save him all his life!

Pray for Laborers

A Scripture flashed across my mind. Jesus said in Matthew 9:38, *"Pray ye therefore the Lord of the harvest, that he will send forth labourers into his harvest."*

I pulled over to the side of the road and stopped the car. I bowed my head and prayed, "Dear Lord, I know it wouldn't do much good if I went and talked to this man, because I know he wouldn't listen to me. But there must be somebody he *will* listen to. I don't know who that is, but You do. Send somebody across his path to witness to him."

Fifteen years of praying, "God save So-and-so" hadn't worked. I prayed one time for God to send a laborer across his path, and within two weeks' time, somebody had crossed his path, prayed with him, and influenced him. Momma told me he bought a Bible and started going to church.

After I had that unusual experience, I started examining the Scriptures. In the church circles I was in then, we always prayed, "God, save the lost. God, save the lost. God, save the lost." But I couldn't find anyplace in the Bible where it said, "Pray for the lost. Pray that God will save sinners."

Instead, I found where Jesus had said, *"Pray ye . . . the Lord of the harvest, that he will send forth labourers into his harvest."* The harvest is there waiting to be harvested. We need laborers.

There is somebody who can talk to your relatives when you can't. You need to realize that.

Believing for a laborer to cross your unsaved loved one's path isn't the only way to get him or her saved, however. You need to listen to your spirit for instructions on how to reach them.

The Role of Prayer

One thing you can do is to intercede on your loved one's behalf.

Often when we pray for our unsaved loved ones, we're trying to make God do something. We're trying to force something to come to pass.

Actually, what we need to do is to study the Word and depend upon and trust in the Spirit of God to do the work. Put the Word of God first. *No prayer life is going to be successful if it's not based on the Word of God.*

Realize that getting the answer may depend on you. The manifestation can come faster if the Word of God is strongly rooted in you. The Bible says, ". . .*faith cometh by hearing, and hearing by the word of God"* (Rom. 10:17). In other words, your faith is stronger if you have a lot of the Word in you.

That's the reason I don't even pray about some things for several days until I have examined the Word carefully on the subject. (Emergencies are different.) If the situation has existed for years and hasn't changed, it's still going to be there in a few days, so you've got time to study what the Word has to say about it. Keep examining the Word. Keep meditating on it.

Sometimes I have gone for days meditating on just one thing. After three or four days, I've found that faith is so strong in me, I could not doubt if I wanted to, because the Word has built something into me!

Jesus said in John 15:7, *"If ye abide in me, and my words abide in you, ye shall ask what ye will, and it shall be done unto you."* You see, it's after the Word of God gets into you that you're able to pray effectively.

Because the Spirit of God knows who can be touched — we don't — He may lead you to intercede for people you barely know instead of your unsaved loved ones or friends.

After a certain period of time, you will find that the burden of prayer will be lifted, and a spirit of lightness will prevail. Sometimes people begin to laugh. Many times I have laughed or sung in the Spirit. Why? When the burden lifts, that means the answer is assured, even though it hasn't been manifested yet.

The Role of Authority

Some years ago, I was studying what the New Testament has to say about the authority of the believer.

I wasn't even thinking about my unsaved relatives. While
reading in Second Corinthians 4, however, I saw where
Paul said that the god of this world, Satan, has blinded
the minds of those who are lost. And I began to understand
something.

An inward something said, "Do you think a sane,
sensible person would drive his car down the highway at
80 to 100 miles an hour, run right by flashing red lights
and signs that said 'Danger Ahead' or 'Bridge Out,' and
run off the road and kill himself?"

I answered out loud, "No, no. I don't think so."

Then I realized that a drunk or doped person would
do this. Why? Because the god of this world had blinded
his mind.

It is a well-known fact that automobile accidents
frequently happen to people who have just had a family
feud or fuss. They aren't paying attention to their driving,
because their minds are befuddled. Similarly, the devil has
blinded the minds of the unsaved, because no rational
human being would rush through life and plunge into hell.

Reading there in Second Corinthians, I began to see
something I had never seen before: *We need to break the
power of the devil over our unsaved loved ones, because
the devil has their minds blinded!*

You need to get this same revelation if it's to work for
you. It won't work for you just because it worked for me.

Any time I receive a revelation from God, I try it out
before I start preaching it. I want to see if it works. If
it won't work for me, how is it going to work for you? The
Bible says, *"Prove all things; hold fast that which is good"*
(1 Thess. 5:21). I'll even try it in the hardest places first;
I won't start on easy ones.

When I saw this truth, I reasoned, *If that's true* (and I knew it was, because it is the Word of God), *if I can make it work on my brother Dub, I can make it work on anybody, because he's the "black sheep" of the family. Many of them are sinners, but he's the worst case. If it will work on Dub, it will work on ANYBODY!*

I had been lying across the bed, studying, when I made this decision. I rose up with my Bible in one hand, and I lifted my other hand to heaven. I said, "In the Name of the Lord Jesus Christ, I break the power of the devil over my brother Dub's life, and I claim his deliverance. That means deliverance from the devil and full salvation in Jesus' Name. Amen."

I had prayed and occasionally fasted for Dub for fifteen years. None of it seemed to work. In fact, Dub seemed to get worse. But once I prayed that prayer, breaking the power of the devil over Dub's life, that settled it for me. I wouldn't even touch it in my thought life; I wouldn't even think about it.

About a week went by. Then one day a voice said to me, "Oh, come on, now. You don't believe old Dub will ever be saved, do you?"

Reason vs. Faith

I started to think about the situation. And this is a critical point on receiving salvation, faith, or whatever you need from God: *As long as Satan can hold you in the arena of REASON, he will whip you every time — in every battle, in every conflict. But if you will hold Satan in the arena of FAITH, you will defeat him every time!*

I started to think about it for a moment. Then I shut

my mind off and wouldn't think about it. (You can train yourself to do that; I started doing it as a teenager.)

From way down inside of me — in my spirit — something sort of bubbled up. It came out of my mouth, and I started laughing — from right out of the inside of me.

I said, "No, no, I don't *think* Dub will be saved — I *know* it. You see, Satan, I took the Name of Jesus (Satan won't argue with you about that Name) and broke your power over Dub and claimed his deliverance — deliverance from Satan and full salvation!"

If the devil could have gotten me started thinking, *Well, I hope he gets saved . . . I don't know whether he will be or not . . . maybe he will* — he would have defeated me. But I just shut my mind off and refused to worry about it.

Within two weeks, Dub was saved. He ended up preaching the gospel until the time he went home to be with the Lord.

Other Methods

This is just one way to pray for the salvation of a loved one. I prayed differently for other relatives.

For one I just said, "Lord, send somebody across his path." For another I said, "I break the power of the devil over him." I had the spirit of intercession for others.

It all comes back to the Word of God and the Spirit of God. Every Christian needs to get into the Word and study what the Bible says on this subject of praying for the lost. For example, Romans 15:1 says, *"We then that are strong ought to bear the infirmities of the weak. . . ."* Galatians 6:2 says, *"Bear ye one another's burdens, and so fulfil the law of Christ."*

Often people pray incorrectly — and they open the door to the devil. They pray, "Lord, bring my loved one in *at any cost.*" But Jesus has already paid the cost! People need to understand that. If you don't, you're opening the door for the devil to do a lot of things. People say, "Well, God used that tragedy to bring him to salvation." But that kind of thinking is not in line with the Bible.

People have gotten saved in times of war when bombs were dropping and innocent women and children were being killed. But that wasn't God's way of bringing them to salvation! Of course, God is there when people turn to Him. But you don't need to pray tragedies on people to make them come to God!

When God begins to deal with a person, a spirit of conviction comes upon him — and it usually comes through prayer. Often he becomes more miserable and more difficult to live with than ever before — but you needn't pray an accident or illness upon him so he will be born again!

Instead, you must depend on the Spirit of God to lead you. You must use wisdom to know when to speak to your unsaved loved ones and when to keep your mouth shut. All the time, of course, you're praying for them.

God Deals With Families

Many people are confused about Acts 16:31: "... *Believe on the Lord Jesus Christ, and thou shalt be saved, and thy house.*" Other translations read, "... and thy house if they believe." You see, you're going to have to get them to believe.

In Acts 16, the Philippian jailer got saved. He was the

head of his house. Once he got saved, he began to do what the Bible says to do: He began to pray and set the right example in front of his household — and they got saved. That's all there is to it.

I never doubted that my whole household would be saved — by this I mean my immediate family. My wife was already saved when we were married, and later we had two children. The thought never occurred to me that my children wouldn't be saved. I knew they would.

God does deal with families, and the man should take the lead. If he doesn't, then the wife will have to. But most of the time, when the man becomes a Christian, walks with God, is the head of his house, prays, and has family devotions, his family will all follow him.

Even though we don't have a lot of Scriptures for it, I thoroughly believe that God deals with families. In the Old Testament, God dealt more with individuals, and we know that under the New Testament He still deals primarily with individuals. However, because God instituted the family, He also deals with families.

Claiming Relatives

When it comes to "claiming" your family, you must do certain things. For example, you must train up a child in the way he should go, Proverbs 22:6 tells us. You must bring a child up in the nurture and admonition of the Lord, we see in Ephesians 6:4. Paul said to Timothy, "... *that from a child thou hast known the holy scriptures ...* " (2 Tim. 3:15). How did Timothy know them? He had to be taught them by his family.

When it comes to an unsaved husband or wife, you

can't always claim that spouse's salvation. If you could, Paul would have said so when he wrote to the Church at Corinth.

What did Paul say? *"And the woman which hath an husband that believeth not, and if he be PLEASED to dwell with her, let her not leave him. . . . But if the unbelieving depart, let him depart. A brother or a sister is not under bondage in such cases . . . "* (1 Cor. 7:13,15).

"Pleased to dwell with her" (or him) means to live with you as a husband or wife — not to run around with everybody in the country.

If you could always claim an unsaved loved one's salvation, Paul would have said so right here, because he was writing by inspiration of the Holy Spirit.

Young people trying to minister to their unsaved parents also need to be led by the Spirit. I know children and teenagers who got saved and then led their parents to the Lord. On the other hand, I know teenagers who got saved and caused a division between themselves and their parents because they pushed things too fast and too hard in witnessing.

The Role of the Will

You can be interested in others and be burdened for them, but you can't lay down ironclad rules and say, "You can claim somebody else's salvation," just because you want them to be saved. Of course, we *want* everybody to be saved, but that other person has something to do with it. A person's will is involved in accepting or rejecting Christ.

Once the power of the devil is broken over people and

they're free to make a choice, they will usually make the right choice. If their mind is blinded, of course, they can't make the right choice. But normally, people will come to the Lord once Satan's power over them is broken. You can't say it will happen one hundred percent of the time, however, because some people just willfully won't follow the Lord!

So we do have guidelines, and most of the time you can discover them by studying the Word. Where there are no guidelines, you must depend on what the Spirit of God tells you to do. But check your motives.

Let the Lord send whom He wills across your unsaved loved ones' paths. Some people are more expert at soul-winning than others. I've noticed that many who are preaching the Full Gospel today didn't get saved in Full Gospel circles; they got saved in fundamentalist or other circles. Later they began to see the light on the baptism in the Holy Spirit and speaking in tongues, and they moved on into Full Gospel circles.

The main thing is to get people saved and get them into heaven! Whether they get healed or not, they can go to heaven if they're saved. In other words, you can go to heaven with a sick body, but you can't go to heaven with a sin-sick spirit. And once you're saved, you can go to heaven whether or not you have the baptism in the Holy Spirit.

Salvation is the important thing!